AF428122

THE GLORY OF THE RENAISSANCE THROUGH ITS PAINTINGS

HISTORY 5th GRADE

Children's Renaissance Books

In this book, we're going to talk about the beautiful painting masterpieces of the Renaissance. So, let's get right to it!

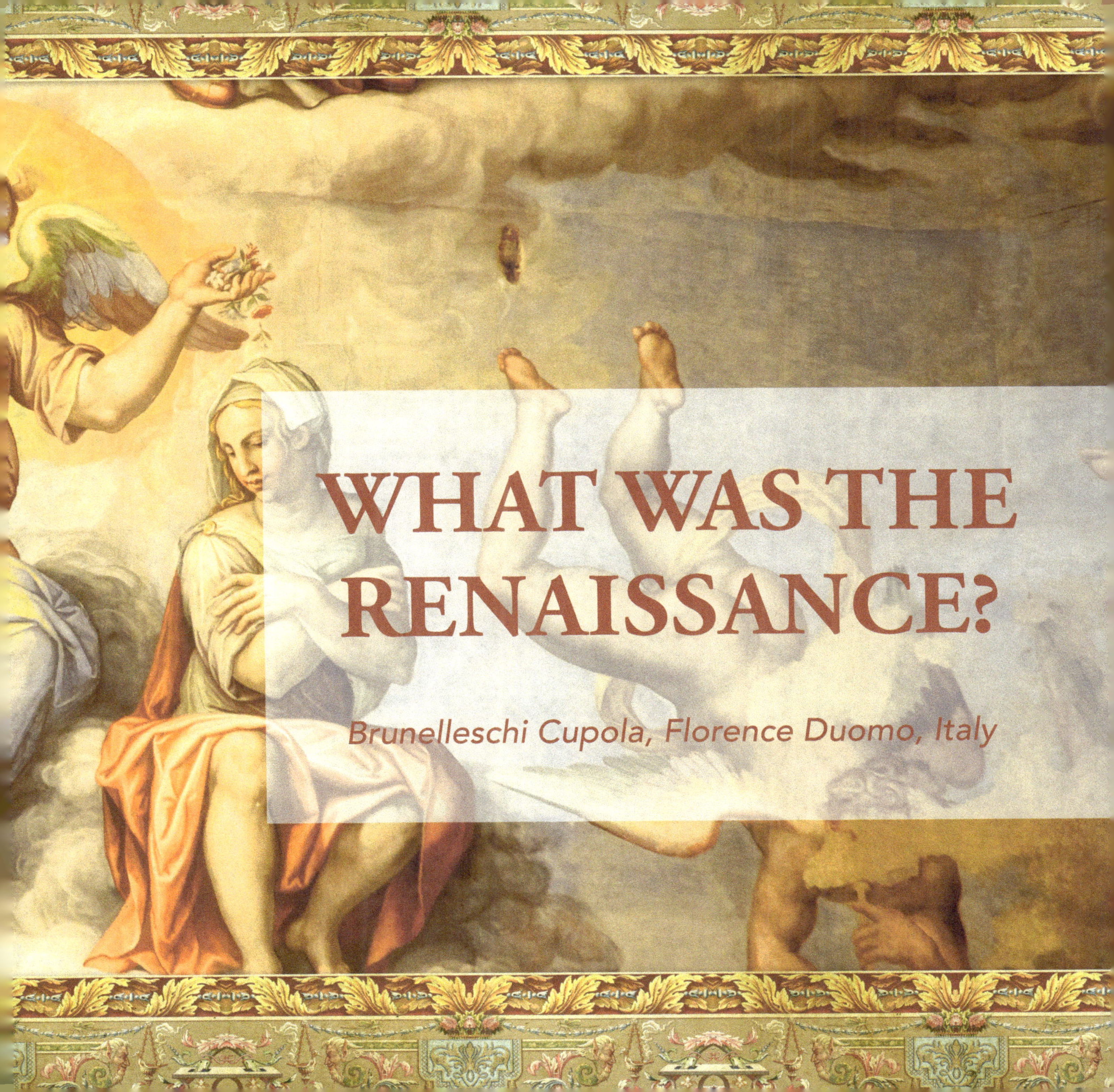

WHAT WAS THE RENAISSANCE?

Brunelleschi Cupola, Florence Duomo, Italy

The Middle Ages was a dark time in Europe. Conditions were unsanitary and most people lived a life of struggle and uncertainty. The Black Death had wiped out millions of people. The Church controlled everything and most people lived in fear of death or the fires of hell. In the midst of this struggle, people longed for a better life.

As Europe transitioned out of the Middle Ages, things began to change. There was a revival of research centered around former glorious civilizations, such as those of Greece and Rome. Although things were still unstable politically, there was more wealth. New machines, such as the printing press, had made reading and literacy available to many more people. As a result, people from all social backgrounds became educated.

Science was beginning to blossom. New frontiers were being discovered both on Earth, such as new continents, and in the newly discovered celestial bodies in the sky. The Humanist philosophy began to emerge. It turned attention away from religion and back to the realism and beauty of mankind and the joys of being human.

D uring the Renaissance, the arts thrived. Poetry, literature, architecture, painting, and sculpting all took huge leaps forward. The style that we identify with the Renaissance today began in the country of Italy in the late part of the 14th century.

It reached its **_"golden age"_** at the end of the 15th century and the early part of the 16th century. This was the time period when there were amazing master painters, such as Leonardo da Vinci as well as Raphael and Michelangelo.

The Tribute Money for the Brancacci by Masaccio.

THE ORIGIN OF RENAISSANCE ART

The beginnings of what we know today as the style of Renaissance art paintings go back to Italy during the time period between 1280 through 1400 AD. This period is now called the *"proto-Renaissance."* It began with admired writers such as Petrarch and Boccaccio. They were scholars of the civilizations of ancient Greece and ancient Rome. They admired the language and traditions of those cultures and wanted them to be revived once more.

This feeling quickly progressed from words to paintings. The most famous painter of the proto-Renaissance was Giotto from Florence. His paintings represented a huge departure from the style of the Middle Ages. In the Middle Ages, the style had a look that was flat-looking and abstract. In this Byzantine style, the religious figures depicted looked more like icons than people.

Giotto began to paint the people and objects in his paintings with a much more realistic style. In addition to painting with more realism, the figures also showed real emotions in their faces as well as their gestures. Giotto's innovations would be refined by later Renaissance artists, but he started a movement that blossomed throughout the Renaissance.

Renaissance Fresco.

THE TEN MOST FAMOUS PAINTINGS OF THE RENAISSANCE

If you study some of the most famous paintings of the Renaissance, you can learn a great deal about this golden age in human history.

Trials and Calling of Moses - Details of Frescos by Sandro Botticelli.

The Kiss of Judas
by Giotto, 1306 AD

Many art historians believe that Giotto was really the first modern painter. The frescoes that he painted on the walls of the Scrovegni Chapel are amazing works by the master painter. The fresco cycle tells stories in different panels. Perhaps the most famous painting in the Chapel is **The Kiss of Judas.** It shows the exact moment when Judas betrays Jesus to the soldiers.

Giotto captured the realism of the chaos in the crowd as Christ is arrested. The expressions on Jesus's face as well as the face of his betrayer, Judas, add emotional power to the painting.

Primavera by Sandro Botticelli

Primavera
by Botticelli, 1482 AD

Sandro Botticelli painted Primavera, which is sometimes called **Allegory of Spring.** This painting shows the Renaissance adoration for the myths of ancient Rome. It depicts figures in a garden, as well as ripe oranges, and a profusion of hundreds of different types of flowers. The goddess of love, Venus, stands in the center, as Cupid flies overhead. Three female figures, possibly Muses, dance together, while a young man raises his hand to pluck an orange.

At the right of Venus, a young woman in a beautiful floral dress, who appears to be a representation of the season of spring, carries a basket of flowers. At the far right, another female figure is being lifted by a male figure from the sky. There are many ways to interpret the painting, which has made it one of the most talked about paintings in the world. Many art historians believe the painting represents the fertility of the world.

The Birth of Venus by Botticelli.

The Birth of Venus

by Botticelli, 1486 AD

A second masterpiece by Botticelli is *The Birth of Venus.* This beautiful painting shows the lovely goddess Venus fully formed as an adult woman as she is born from the sea. She stands on a seashell with the wind blowing through her hair. She is blown toward the approaching shoreline by Zephyrus, who is the god of the winds, and Aura, the breeze goddess.

At her right, the Hora of Spring is standing on dry land and is ready to cover Venus's nudity with a luxurious cloak, decorated with the abundant flowers of spring. The winds shower Venus with roses. According to mythology, the rose blossomed for the first time when Venus was born. Venus inspired men and women to enjoy physical love and from that experience to connect with divine love. This philosophy is called Neoplatonic love.

The Last Supper by Da Vinci.

# The Last Supper

by Leonardo da Vinci, 1498 AD

In this huge 15-foot tall by 29-foot wide painting that covers the wall in a convent dining room, Leonardo painted the confusion among the twelve disciples when they realize the impact of what Jesus is saying. Over their Passover supper, he is telling them that one of them is about to betray him. Every face in the painting was modeled after a real person.

Leonardo used his advanced knowledge of anatomy to draw the figures in lifelike poses during this dramatic moment of their final meal with Jesus. Unfortunately, because of the method Leonardo used to create the painting, this masterpiece had deteriorated over the many centuries. A 20-year-long restoration of the painting sought to return it to its former glory, but it has been controversial since not much of the original paint remains.

The School of Athens
by Raphael, 1511 AD

The ***School of Athens*** is one of four frescoes that Raphael painted for the Vatican's Apostolic Palace. The four paintings are meant to depict important areas of study during ancient Greek civilization—the study of philosophy, the study of poetry, the study of God and religious beliefs, also called Theology, and the study of law.

The School of Athens by Raphael (engrave etching of the original).

This painting depicted Greek philosophy and the two central figures in the painting are Plato and Aristotle as well as 19 other philosophers. The painting embodies the reverence Renaissance culture had for the classical periods of Greece and Rome.

The Sistine Madonna

by Raphael, 1512 AD

The *Sistine Madonna* by the prolific painter Raphael shows the Virgin Mary holding the Baby Jesus in her arms as she faces forward standing in the clouds. Saint Sixtus kneels before them on one side and Saint Barbara does the same on the other side as she casts her eyes down toward the cherubs.

Raphael - The Sistine Madonna.

As you view the painting, you can almost imagine you are in heaven, until you see the whimsical two cherubs at the bottom of the painting. They look wistfully upwards at Mary and Jesus. Raphael painted hundreds of paintings in his lifetime, and this masterpiece has been claimed as **"*divine*"** by many art critics.

The Creation of Adam
by Michelangelo, 1512 AD

Michelangelo did not think of himself as a painter. In his mind, he was a sculptor. However, when Pope Julius II strongly requested that he paint the Sistine Chapel's ceiling, he reluctantly began the work. At the beginning, the work was supposed to be a painting of the twelve apostles, but Michelangelo chose depictions from the Old Testament instead, namely the book of Genesis.

The Creation of Adam by Michelangelo.

Of all the paintings, the masterpiece that is most recognized is the scene called *The Creation of Adam.* Here, God extends his finger to touch Adam's and give him consciousness. In fact, some have suggested that the shape Michelangelo drew behind God depicts a brain to show that the Creator is giving life and intelligence to mankind.

The Mona Lisa
by Leonardo da Vinci, 1517 AD

Leonardo da Vinci did not complete many paintings in his lifetime, but one of the masterpieces he did complete that retains its original beauty is the **Mona Lisa.** More than likely the piece was commissioned and it was supposed to be a portrait of the wife of a wealthy silk merchant.

Close-up of the Mona Lisa by Leonardo da Vinci.

However, Leonardo couldn't give it up. Perhaps he felt in his heart that it was priceless. The lady with the mysterious smile has been written and sung about and even made fun of, but today she is worth about $1 billion dollars and hangs in the Louvre in Paris.

# The Assumption of the Virgin

by Titian, 1518 AD

The ***Assumption of the Virgin*** by Titian was the first painting Titian was commissioned to do in Venice and it quickly established him as a master painter. The painting shows Mary rising up to heaven on clouds surrounded by angels as the apostles look up in awe.

Assumption of the Virgin.

The Last Judgement
by Michelangelo, 1541 AD

The *Last Judgement* by Michelangelo was painted twenty-five years after he completed the paintings for the ceiling of the Sistine Chapel. This painting is on the altar wall and shows a powerful and dynamic figure of Christ at his Second Coming as he judges those who will go to hell and those who will go to heaven.

The Last Judgement by Michelangelo.

IONAS

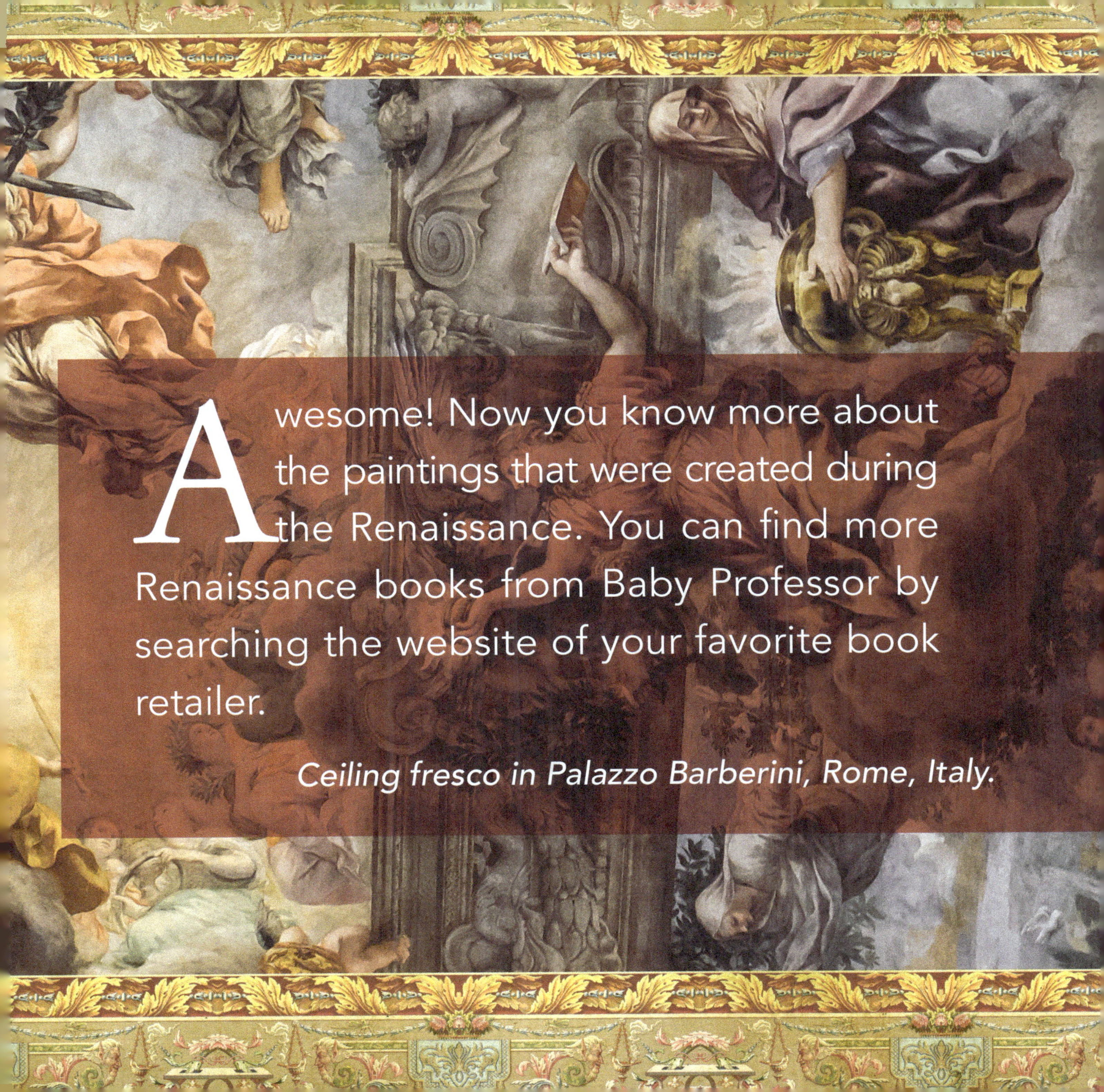

Awesome! Now you know more about the paintings that were created during the Renaissance. You can find more Renaissance books from Baby Professor by searching the website of your favorite book retailer.

Ceiling fresco in Palazzo Barberini, Rome, Italy.

Visit
BABY PROFESSOR
EDUCATION KIDS
www.BabyProfessorBooks.com
to download Free Baby Professor eBooks
and view our catalog of new and exciting
Children's Books